God made us all Different!

Written by Judy Billing
Illustrated by Olha Tkachenko

Dedicated to my dearest friend Margery.
Forever in my heart

God made us all different!
Billing, Judy - author, 2021
Illustrations , layout & design by Olha Tkachenko, Little Big Me
Publishing, 2021   WWW.LITTLEBIG.ME
ISBN: 978-1-7776036-0-1

Luke 6:37

Do not judge and you will not be judged.

God made us all so different;
That's oh, so very true.
No two people are the same;
There's just one me and you.

He made us different sizes;
Some are short and some are tall.
Some are very, very big;
And some are very, very small.

He made us different colours,
Such a lovely thing to see.
Jesus loves all of the colours,
Some like you and some like me.

Judy's face has lots of freckles.
Lindsay Jane does not have one.
Judy's daddy says her freckles
Are just kisses from the sun.

We're all so very different.
Grandma says we all belong.

It doesn't mean one way is right
And the other way is wrong.

Jesus tells us, "Do not judge."
For that's not the thing to do.
For He says if we judge others,
Then God will judge us, too.

Jeannie's hair is short and curly.
Betty's hair is straight and long.
Cindy always wears a ball cap
As she whistles out a song.

Harry's really good at dancing;
He may one day be a star.
Bobby's on the football team;
His coach says he will go far!

Sally likes to play with games.
Her big brother likes to bake.
You can find him in the kitchen,
Putting icing on a cake.

We're all so very different.
Grandma says we all belong.
It doesn't mean one way is right
And the other way is wrong.

Jesus tells us, "Do not judge."
For that's not the thing to do.
For He says if we judge others,
Then God will judge us, too.

Lainey likes to entertain us;
How she loves to dance and sing!
Mikey's very, very shy;
Entertaining's not his thing.

Rosie likes to sleep in late.
Barbie's up before the sun.

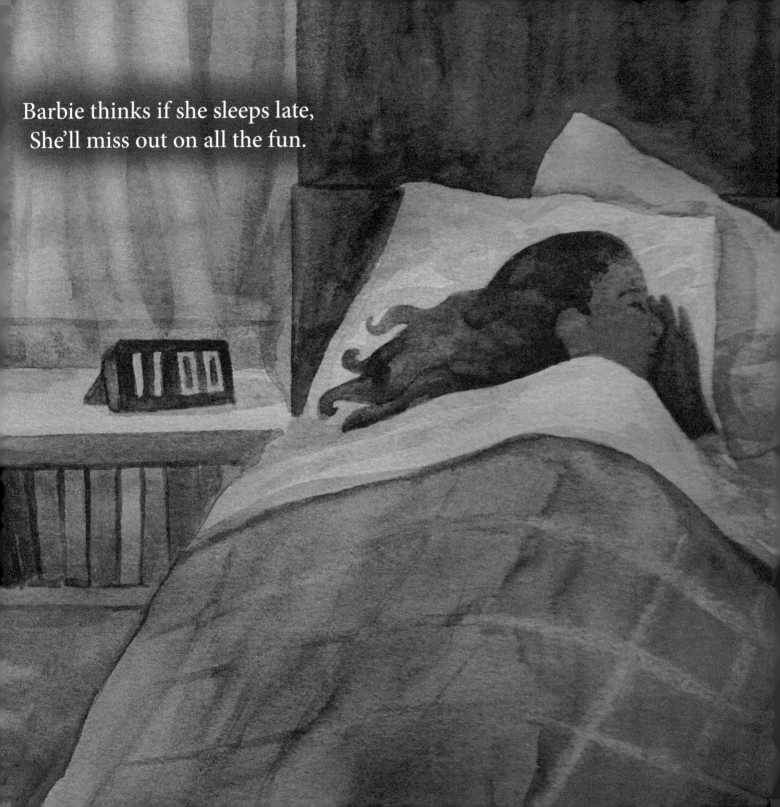

Barbie thinks if she sleeps late,
She'll miss out on all the fun.

Dillon likes to read good books,
And he'd rather be alone.
Susie likes to be with friends,
Or she's talking on her phone.

We're all so very different.
Grandma says we all belong.
It doesn't mean one way is right
And the other way is wrong.

Jesus tells us, "Do not judge."
For that's not the thing to do.
For He says if we judge others,
Then God will judge us, too.

Billy's words are sometimes bouncy
When he's asked to speak out loud.
While Georgia likes to talk a lot,
Especially in a crowd.

Carla has to walk with crutches.
Johnny runs out in the hall.
Teacher has to always ask him,
"Please slow down before you fall!"

There are children in this world,
Who may be very poor.
They have to wear the same clothes
That they wore the day before.

Jesus tells us not to judge them,
For they're just like you and me.
We were all created equal,
Just different, don't you see?

It's not about our shape,
Or our colour, or our size.
It's not if we are rich or poor,
Or if we lose or win the prize.

It's not if we act silly,
Or we're really, really smart.
It's about our love for others
And the love that's in our heart!

Jesus loves all of the children;
He loves me and He loves you.
And it makes Him very happy
When we love each other, too!

We are not to judge each other,
And we know that's very true.
Grandma tells us to remember
What Jesus says to me and you.

Jesus tells us, "Do not judge."
For that's not the thing to do.
For He says if we judge others,
Then God will judge us, too.
Amen!

CPSIA information can be obtained
at www.ICGtesting.com
Printed in the USA
LVHW071728260421
685609LV00010B/208